Canaries

J. Bernacki

© T.F.H. Publications, Inc.

Distributed in the UNITED STATES to the Pet Trade by T.F.H. Publications, Inc., 1 TFH Plaza, Neptune City, NJ 07753; on the Internet at www.tfh.com; in CANADA by Rolf C. Hagen Inc., 3225 Sartelon St., Montreal, Quebec H4R 1E8; Pet Trade by H & L Pet Supplies Inc., 27 Kingston Crescent, Kitchener, Ontario N2B 2T6; in ENGLAND by T.F.H. Publications, PO Box 74, Havant PO9 5TT; in AUSTRALIA AND THE SOUTH PACIFIC by T.F.H. (Australia), Pty. Ltd., Box 149, Brookvale 2100 N.S.W., Australia; in NEW ZEALAND by Brooklands Aquarium Ltd., 5 McGiven Drive, New Plymouth, RD1 New Zealand; in SOUTH AFRICA by Rolf C. Hagen S.A. (PTY.) LTD., P.O. Box 201199, Durban North 4016, South Africa; in JAPAN by T.F.H. Publications. Published by T.F.H. Publications, Inc.

MANUFACTURED IN THE
UNITED STATES OF AMERICA
BY T.F.H. PUBLICATIONS, INC.

Contents

Photography by: Dr. Herbert Axelrod, John Bernacki, Isabelle Francais, Michael Gilroy, Ray Hunziker, H. Lacey, Horst Mayer, Robert Pearcy, Mervin F. Roberts, Maleta Walls, and Jerry Walls.

What is a Canary?

The canary is a small bird that has been domesticated since the 17th century. It is a finch and is available in a variety of colors and shapes. It is an active, cheerful, colorful creature requiring a minimum amount of care and is therefore appropriate as a pet or a companion for those just beginning in the hobby. Canaries originally were captured in the wild and kept for their delightful song. Through careful selection and breeding, that original song was perfected to a multitude of pleasing arias.

Unlike a dog or cat, a canary is best kept in a caged environment constantly supplied with food and water. Although canaries can be tamed to some degree, they are not as easily tamed as the hookbills (i.e. parakeets, parrot-like birds), nor can they mimic words or other sounds.

Before you decide to purchase a canary, you will have to decide if you want one for its song, or merely to have a colorful, active pet to entertain you and your family for hours on end.

WHAT TO EXPECT

Although canaries are somewhat delicate, they are a lot tougher than most people think. Of course, you can't wrestle with one as you would a Labrador Retriever or Boxer, but you can interact with one. Their small size makes them fragile, and like all animals they cannot withstand poor nutrition and cage keeping, lack of adequate exercise, inconsistent lighting or temperature, and excessive noise or other threatening happenings. The statement is sometimes made that "My canary died from a draft." Obviously, this may be true if a canary is not in its best condition due to any one, or a combination, of the above. However, a canary that is fed a nutritious diet and is well taken care of will withstand an occasional draft with minor health problems. Several years ago I experienced a terrible ice storm and lost electrical power for several weeks. Because my canaries were in such super condition they were able to survive the brutal cold. One of the objectives of this book is to show the potential pet owner or breeder the proper way to maintain one or more canaries so that they can live a long and healthy life.

The canary has been domesticated since the 17th century. It is available in a variety of colors. Yellow is the most popular color of choice.

Selecting the Right Canary

In choosing the canary you would like to have as a pet you will have to decide what kind of bird you really want. Are you primarily interested in a songster? If so, is it one that sings loudly, or one that sings softly? Does it matter to you if the bird only chirps and does not sing? Do you like a particular color? Many people believe that all canaries are yellow. While that may be a popular color, canaries are available in a multitude of colors including red, white, green, tan, and gray. These colors can be variegated, which is a combination of light and dark colors. Some canaries have crests on their heads while others have different feather lengths and shapes.

Shoppers should purchase their canary from a reliable breeder or reputable pet store. Such breeders can be located through a local bird club or a national specialty club. If you choose to purchase from a pet or bird store, shop around and be sure to find one that does an excellent job selecting and caring for their stock. These establishments will also provide guarantees for health and singing. The buyer should take every step to ensure that he or she is dealing with a reliable seller, be it breeder or pet store.

WHAT NOT TO DO

Do not buy a bird sight unseen. If you want a singing canary as a pet, pick out a bird that is actually singing. Only male canaries sing. Make sure that the bird's eyes are round, clear, and bright. Look at the droppings in the cage. The droppings should be firm, containing white and black areas. Droppings that are spread out, watery, or green colored indicate that the bird is ill. Get as close to the cage as you can and listen carefully. There should be no wheezing, gurgling, or any other sound when the bird breathes. The nostrils should be clean and have no discharge of any type. Feathers should be tight and clean. In addition, the bird's body should be completely filled out with feathers. Never buy a bird that is in molt—its annual loss and renewal of feathers. This is a stressful time and the canary should be allowed to complete its molt before being changed from its existing surroundings. The vent (the excretion area) should be clean. Note the feet as well; they should be clean and smooth with no trace of scales or other growths. A swollen abdomen usually indicates a female that is in breeding condition or has already been bred that season. There should be a closed ring or band on one of its legs indicating the year it hatched and other information traceable to its breeder. Always buy a bird that was hatched in the year you are purchasing it. This is the best policy for the beginner.

WHAT IF?

What if the bird you buy does not sing when you get it home? Allow at least a week to pass before becoming discouraged. If the bird still does not sing, return it for an exchange or refund. Too many times, buyers will become attached to the pet and become reluctant to return it. If you wanted a singing canary you should have one. That is why a written singing guarantee should be obtained from the seller at the time of purchase. There should also be a health guarantee.

Choose your canary from a reputable pet store that takes pride in selling healthy stock.

Setting Up: Equipment, Location and Food

Before bringing a canary home, you should have the cage set up and all the other accessories in advance. The best way to care for a canary is to be prepared before you make a purchase. Talk to other canary owners for honest input. Breeders and bird clubs are also good sources of information, and there are plenty of books available for the beginner. It is extremely important that you understand in advance all, or most, of what is required to successfully take care of your canary.

EQUIPMENT

The most important piece of equipment you will purchase is the cage. Try to obtain the largest one that you can afford with the bar spacing small enough to prevent the

Canaries require a cage large enough to provide ample exercise. Remember that it must have the bar spacing close enough so that the canary cannot escape.

The accessories that you assemble your canary's cage with should be safe, non-toxic and easy to maintain.

bird from escaping. It is absolutely cruel to keep a bird confined in a very small cage. I usually recommend a cage that is long enough for the bird to obtain a minimum of exercise. The smallest size that I would use is 15 inch x 10 inch x 14 inch high. Other criteria that may alter your decision are the cost and space restrictions where the cage will be kept. Because canaries and other birds feel more secure at higher elevations, it is suggested that the cage be hung from a floor stand, from a wall bracket, or from the ceiling. In all of these possibilities the cage should be at a height where your access to food and water

5

containers is easy. Brass- or chrome-plated cages are generally preferred because they are easy to clean, and the plating materials are typically very permanent. Paint is accepted only if it is lead free; make sure that you get this assurance before making any purchase. Finally, do not purchase a wooden or bamboo cage; they are difficult to disinfect and become a haven for mites and other similar pests.

Whatever cage you purchase, it will require perches, seed and treat cups, a water drinker, cuttlebone, and some other accessories.

The canary is a small creature that is totally dependent on its owner for good care. It is therefore important that the very best equipment that you can afford be purchased.

While inquiring about canary cages, it's a good idea to look for cages that are designed with sloped surfaces to catch debris in the tray, and not your floor. Smooth, rounded corners not only help for easy cleaning, but can provide a safe environment that won't harm you or your bird. A good cage will also come with a grate and tray that slides out easily, while a decorative or cabinet stand to place underneath the cage can be added on separately. Photo courtesy of Animal Environments.

Fresh greens are an important part of your canary's diet. They should be washed thoroughly and fed on a regular basis.

Left: *Canaries almost always relish greens and carrot pieces. It is important that these be discarded from the cage if not eaten because they quickly spoil.*

Like other birds, a canary's diet should consist of a wide variety of fruits, vegetables, and seeds; for added nutrition, many seed diets are fortified with vitamins, minerals, and amino acids. Supplemental products such as egg-based foods and song foods are also available. Photo courtesy of Sun Seed Company, Inc.

Perches should be wooden and of varying sizes so that the bird can constantly change the position of its feet. Compare your canary's perches to the natural perches of the wild birds outside. Their perches are twigs, branches, and whatever else they can grab on to. No one branch or twig is the same as the next. This is why perches with at least two different diameters should be mounted in your canary's cage. You may also choose to run a very coarse hacksaw blade down the length of each perch so that each perch has linear grooves running from one end to the other. This allows the bottoms of their feet to be exposed to air, and prevents difficulties.

The use of sandpaper perch covers is very abrasive to the bottom of a bird's feet. Although they are regarded as tools for keeping toenails from growing too long, they cause the bottoms of the feet to become very sore, and they are best not used.

A water dispenser is also required. My dispenser of choice is a glass tube with a small plastic bottom. The tube stays on the outside when the plastic bottom is mounted between the cage wires. This makes changes easy. Note that water and the water tube should be changed and cleaned daily. Sometimes, food gets into the water and can spoil the quality of the water. This is especially true during warm weather and even more so if water-soluble vitamins are being used.

You will also need a good mineral grit that should be made available in a cup or some other container, along with a piece of cuttlebone hanging in the cage. Both provide the minerals that may be missing in the daily diet, and the bird will use them as needed. Toys or other sorts of entertainment should also be included in the cage. A commercial product composed of a bunch of stiff "hairs" is enjoyed by most birds; some of these have a small bell in them that arouses additional curiosity. Sometimes a swing is likewise enjoyed, sometimes not; it depends on the size of the cage and your canary's preferences.

The cage floor should have clean paper on the bottom, either newsprint, white paper towels, or paper bags are recommended. Newsprint is the paper that is used to print newspapers but without any print on it. At one time, many advocated the use of newspapers. This recommendation has changed for several reasons: (1) The inks and solvents may be more toxic than in the past, and air aging may not allow the offending chemicals to evaporate thus putting your bird at jeopardy; (2) the inks transfer to the birds making them appear dirty. Paper towels are commonly available; stacking about one week's worth of paper on the bottom of the cage and removing the top layer daily, makes cleanup a breeze.

Your canary will enjoy bathing, and many types of

Any additional foodstuffs that you give to your pet canary should be free of pesticides and non-toxic.

To thrive, birds need to eat the kind of variety of foods they'd find in their natural environment—vegetables, nuts, grains and fruits—the fresher the better. Photo courtesy of Eight in One Pet Products, Inc.

When more than one bird is housed in a cage or flight, be sure to provide enough food and treats so that fights do not occur.

Your canary needs exercise in addition to a well-balanced diet. Exercise treats are consumable toys that encourage pet activity and help prevent pet boredom. Photo courtesy of Sun Seed Company, Inc.

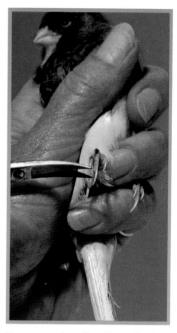

Your canary's nails will need to be trimmed on a regular basis. If you are unable to perform this task, bring your pet to a reliable shop or a veterinarian.

bathtubs and or bathing devices are available. Some hang on the outside of the cage, some are miniature bathtubs that sit on the cage floor. Even small glass ashtrays work out very well. If a bird is hesitant to use a bath, a floating piece of greens in the water usually will entice him.

Many canary owners find seed catchers to be very useful in helping to prevent the scattering of seeds, hulls, and other debris out of the cage. Typically a sewn cloth that covers the bottom half of the cage, a seed catcher is attached by hooks or an elastic band. Although most cages on the market today incorporate plastic side shields, a seed catcher provides that extra measure of protection to help keep your home clean.

Although unable to play as a dog or cat, your canary will become a very valuable member of the family and you will want to acquire the very best cages and accessories.

11

Most canaries enjoy a bath. A shallow tub or dish on the bottom of the cage with cool water will make your canary happy.

Other items that will be needed include a spare cage, mite spray, and medications. The spare cage will be used to house the bird while you are giving the everyday cage a thorough washing. It should be small enough to be used to transport the bird. A can of pyrethrin mite spray is also good to have on hand and can be purchased at most pet stores or in the pet department of a supermarket. Your bird's medicine chest should contain alcohol for wiping off blood; a topical antibiotic, gauze and tape for wounds; oral antibiotic (erythromycin, ampicillin, nystatin) for infections; something for diarrhea; Epsom salts to relieve binding; scissors, nail clippers, toothpicks, and a styptic stop powder.

It is probably best to bring the cage that you will keep the canary in with you when you go to pick up the bird to bring it home. The cage should have the seed and mineral grit containers filled. Don't fill the water tube until you arrive at home as most of the water will probably spill out in moving the cage. Most sellers usually put the bird in a small cardboard box for transport, putting less stress on the bird. When you bring the cage with you, however, the canary can be put directly into it and it doesn't have to be handled anymore. Before leaving the building, cover the cage with a dark cloth—if it is cold outside a blanket may be the better choice. Carry the cage very carefully. Have a location for the cage picked out in advance. Carefully uncover the cage, install the water tube drinker, and place the cage in the location that you have selected.

LOCATION AND SETTLING IN

The best location for your canary's cage is in a relatively quiet area where the canary can see what is going on but where he will not be constantly disturbed by a lot of (people) traffic. It should be placed preferably near an inside wall or where the temperature is fairly constant. I do not recommend placing

12

the cage immediately next to a window as the temperature varies too much. Also, there is a possibility of it becoming overheated if there is no relief from the sun.

It is very important to leave the bird alone for the next two or three days to allow it to become accustomed to its new surroundings. Cover the cage with a dark cloth each night at the same time and uncover it in the morning keeping this time as consistent as possible. Provide clean water and fresh seed the first thing in the morning. By doing this you won't be as likely to forget. Treats, condition food, and vegetation can be given throughout the day. You will notice that the canary will sing the first thing in the morning and throughout the day especially when he hears sounds of running water, the vacuum cleaner, or the refrigerator. Music from the radio or recordings can be played anytime during the day, and there are recordings of canaries' singing to help your bird improve his song. You will find that as time goes by your canary will become less intimidated by you and you may actually be able to have it eat from your hand or perform some other tricks. Remember that this takes an extreme amount of patience, but it is well worth the effort.

Allow your canary to settle in for the first few days in his new surroundings and he will slowly become accustomed to his new cage and accessories.

Canaries can sometimes be enticed to sing when other noises are going on such as the vacuum cleaner, running water, or even the song of another canary.

General Nutrition

nutrition of seed eating birds. My thanks to Kevin Gorman for helping me develop this section.

Proteins are any of a group of complex organic compounds that contain amino acids (nitrogen-containing compounds) as their basic structural units. They occur in all living matter and are essential for the growth and repair of animal tissue.

Proteins are also essential for proper feather formation and feather condition; regulation of water balance (an early sign of protein deficiency is edema, or swelling of the tissues); proper balance of blood pH; healthy immune system (to fight off

Before diving into what we should feed our canary, it is important to have a basic understanding of nutritional science. When addressing the subject of nutrition of all creatures, six basic categories need to be considered: proteins, carbohydrates, fats, vitamins, minerals, and water. This section describes these categories from an avian nutrition viewpoint. Since the subject of this book is canaries, I will focus on the

To visibly improve color and vitality, trust your bird's diet to thoroughly researched and quality-tested foods. Ask your veterinarian about specialty care diets that are also available. Photo courtesy of Roudybush, Inc.

14

Although you cannot force your canary to eat an exact amount of certain foods, you can offer the correct proportions of a good diet.

infections); and absorption of nutrients from the diet.

Proteins are broken down into amino acids by the process of digestion. Animal proteins are complete proteins. They contain all the essential amino acids needed for growth and maintenance. The most complete protein is the egg. Other animal sources of protein for feeding birds are mealworms, insects, and meat. Proteins from vegetable sources are

Right: *The feeding of one bird to another is often only done when young are present or mating is commencing.*

Below: *Some greens have very little nutritional value. As a general rule, the lighter the green, the less nutritional value. Greens such as spinach and escarole have higher nutritional values and are therefore healthier for birds.*

incomplete proteins. These must be complemented by other foods to obtain a complete protein diet.

In the chart below, any item from Group 1 added to breakdown, and birds will be unable to maintain body mass. Complex carbohydrates are broken down into simple sugars (e.g., glucose) in the digestive tract.

Fats and oils are essential for proper insulation, healthy skin and glossy feathers. Waterproofing of the feathers is obtained from an oil gland located at the base of the tail.

Group 1	Group 2	Group 3
Beans/ Legumes	Seeds/Nuts	Grains
Soybeans	Rape Seed	Canary
Lentils	Sunflower Seed	Oat Groats
Peas	Niger Seed	Millet
Peanuts	Hemp Seed	Wheat Germ
		Bread
		Corn

Group 2 or 3 will increase the quality of protein available to the bird. As a rule, the darker the seed, the higher the protein and oil content will be. The best source of protein (from nutrition, cost, and ease-of-use points of view) is egg food. Egg food is a combination of cooked egg and other ingredients that can be used as a supplement, a nestling food (also hand feeding), and a weaning diet.

Carbohydrates are any of a group of chemical compounds, including sugars, starches, and cellulose, containing carbon, hydrogen, and oxygen only, with the ratio of hydrogen to oxygen atoms of usually two to one. Carbohydrates are essential for energy and to maintain body tissue as they are used by the body as an energy source before proteins. A deficiency of carbohydrates will result in muscle tissue and fat

As a general rule, the lighter colored the seed, the more carbohydrate the seed contains. Some exceptions are sesame and safflower which are oil seeds.

Fats are essential in the diet for the absorption of vitamins A, D, E, and K—all fat-soluble vitamins. Fats are also needed for proper growth, sexual development, and reproduction.

Sources of Carbohydrates

Complete Carbohydrates	Simple Carbohydrates
(Starches)	(Sugars)
Oats	Fruits
Millet	Honey
Canary Seed	Table Sugar
Bread Crumbs	Syrup
Corn/Cornbread	

Fats are the most efficient forms of energy storage. The energy value of a food is determined by its calorie content. Fats and oils have twice the calorie content as do proteins and carbohydrates: Protein, four calories/gram; carbohydrate, four cal/g; fat/oil, nine cal/g. Most cage birds in smaller cages do not need much fat or oil in the diet. Too much fat leads to obesity and liver problems. Birds that use large amounts of energy need increased levels of fat in their diet; for example, growing or young birds, molting birds, birds in flight cages, and birds under other stresses.

Fats in the diet are broken down into glycerol and fatty acids. The only fatty acid required in the diet is linoleic acid (from unsaturated fats). All other fatty acids are manufactured within the body.

Minerals are needed for proper bone development, feather development, healthy blood, and egg shell formation. Calcium and phosphorous are required in relatively large amounts.

It can be beneficial to choose a cage with a feeding system already installed. These easy-to-use feeders help to prevent droppings in food and water, which eliminates contamination. External feeders can also provide more room in the enclosure for your pet, while not allowing escapes during feedings. They can be very easily maintained with just the touch of a finger. Photo courtesy of Animal Environments.

Calcium is a major part of bones, eggshell, and muscle. Phosphorous is important in the metabolism of fats and carbohydrates. Other minerals required in relatively large amounts are sodium, potassium, magnesium, iron, and zinc. Magnesium is an essential constituent of bone and eggshells. Potassium is primarily found in the cells of the body, including bone. It plays an important part in the metabolism. Sodium as sodium chloride is usually found in body fluids. It helps keep the body from becoming

Sources of Fats/Oils	
Unsaturated Fats = Oils (liquid at room temp.)	Saturated Fats (solid at room temp.)
Hemp Seed	Coconut Oil
Safflower	Palm Kernel Oil
Sesame	Animal Fats (Lard)
Niger	Butter/Cream
Sunflower	
Rape (Canola)	
All Nuts	

Fats and oils are essential to your canary's diet for proper insulation, healthy skin and glossy feathers.

Greens are essential to a bird's diet in small amounts.

soluble and water-soluble. The fat-soluble vitamins include A, D_3, and K. The water-soluble vitamins are thiamin (B_1), riboflavin (B_2), niacin, pantothenic acid, folic acid, biotin, and C. Deficiencies of vitamins in the diet cause poor health, fertility, and growth.

Vitamin A is probably the most important vitamin in the diet. However, too much vitamin A is toxic so care must be taken not to overdose. Beta carotene is a precursor to vitamin A; in other words, the body can manufacture vitamin A directly from this carotenoid without the danger of overdosing. Vitamin A is heat

too acidic and, with calcium and potassium, is essential for heart activity.

Other minerals needed in smaller amounts are copper, cobalt, iodine, selenium, and chromium. Iron is the main part of hemoglobin; iron and copper together, along with some enzymes, are necessary for egg production. Details of the importance of others can be found in most nutrition books.

Vitamins are needed for the proper metabolism of foods and for maintaining healthy tissue, but they are only required in very small amounts. There are two categories of vitamins: fat

If you feel that your canary is not getting the proper diet, you can give extra vitamins to your bird in his drinking water. These can be purchased from your local bird store.

sensitive and can be destroyed in cooking and baking.

Vitamin D is important for the absorption of calcium and phosphorous resulting in strong bones and the formation of eggshells. In the wild, birds synthesize vitamin D from sunlight; birds kept indoors do not have this advantage, therefore supplementation is necessary.

Vitamin E is necessary for strength and fertility. Normally not a problem with whole seedeaters, it can be increased by supplementation during breeding season.

Unlike parrots, canaries and other finch-like birds do not need to gnaw on wood for good health.

Left: *Fresh, clean drinking water is essential to your canary at all times. Offer bottled water to your bird if you are uncertain of the additives in your city water.*

Below: *Always be certain that the foods and greens that you give your canary are safe and non-poisonous. When in doubt, leave it out.*

Vitamin	Signs of Deficiency	Sources
A	Ruffled plumage, weakness, tremors	Beta Carotene (non-toxic), carrots, leafy greens, corn, cod liver oil, egg yolk. **Dangerous** in excess amounts (toxic only as retinol)
D	Broken bones, rickets, sunlight, thin shelled eggs	Ultraviolet fraction of sunlight, animal oils, preen gland, direct sunlight, eggs
E	Nervous tremors, muscle weakness, infertility	Seed germ in whole seeds
K	Excessive bleeding	Intestinal flora
C	Most birds are unlikely to need	Synthesized from glucose in the liver
B Complex	Poor appetite, poor development, muscle weakness, paralysis, poor feathering, decreased egg production, reduced hatch rate	
B1		Cereal grains
B2		Cereal seeds
Pantothenic Acid		Green leafy plants
Biotin		Green leafy plants, peanuts, eggs
Choline		Fish meal and oils, soybean meal
Folic acid		Green leafy vegetables, seeds

Vitamin K is important in blood clotting and is produced naturally by natural bacteria, called flora, in the intestines. The flora can be destroyed by use of antibiotics.

Deficiencies in any of the B complex vitamins can produce a number of serious defects as indicated in the chart. Vitamin B_1 (thiamin), B_2 (riboflavin), niacin, B_6 (pyridoxine), Vitamin B_3 (pantothenic acid), biotin, choline and folic acid are all essential B vitamins. They provide an appetite and correct certain types of nerve and muscle weaknesses. Vitamin B_{12} helps metabolize carbohydrate, fat and protein and is generally a good overall tonic.

It is thought that seedeaters do not require vitamin C; conversely, the natural acquisition via fruits and vegetables is not harmful.

There are many types of supplements available on the market today. Read directions carefully and use common sense. Always use fresh vitamin supplements and store according to directions. Water soluble multiple vitamins and a multiple vitamin/mineral mix for dry feeding are excellent supplements available at fine pet shops.

Your canary's good health and good looks will be directly related to the diet he consumes.

Daily Routine

FOOD

Each day discard any of the canary seed mixture that is left over from the previous day and replace with one tablespoon of fresh mix. The canary seed mix that I use is a blend of 70 percent canary seed and 30 percent canola seed (also called rape seed). This is the basic diet. You can also use a vitamized seed mixture in lieu of the canary seed mix. Many fine shops now sell seed mixes that have had special processes done to penetrate the vitamins into the seed itself. The basic diet is supplemented with song food mix and a conditioning food mix. The song food mix, composed mostly of oily seeds like niger and flax, stimulates the canary to sing. A conditioning food provides the extra nutrients that a canary

Your canary should have fresh greens supplied as a regular part of his diet.

The basic diet of your canary will be canary seed. It is essential that the seed mix you purchase for your bird is at least 60 to 70 percent of this vital seed.

needs to complete its basic diet. Alternate the song and conditioning foods on a daily basis providing about one-half of a treat cup at each feeding. Treat cups are sometimes called finger cups because they are about the size of a pinkie finger from the tip to the first knuckle. There are also pelleted diets that are becoming more popular; I have had mixed results, but fanciers have had good luck with these "complete" diets.

WATER

Fresh water supplied daily is a must. Always check to make sure that the bird has water. If you suspect that your water source is not good, you can try bottled or distilled water. Realize that distilled water doesn't contain any minerals, and these will therefore have to be supplemented. Water-soluble vitamins can be added to the water to make sure that the diet is not vitamin deficient. It is imperative to frequently change the water especially when water-soluble vitamins are used.

SUPPLEMENTS

Each day the canary should be given small pieces of fruits (peach, apple, pear), vegetables (raw or cooked carrot, cooked potato, corn), and dark greens (endive, spinach, kale, escarole). The feeding of these are spread out throughout the day. You can also feed small pieces of waffle or pancake, cooked egg, cooked chicken or turkey, or unsweetened cereal; cheese, yogurt, or peanut butter are also allowed. Use small amounts. Consider the size of the bird and the proportions of food items. Seeding grasses are a special treat; just make sure that the ground that they come from is not contaminated with poisons, petroleum products or chemical waste. Soaked seed is also relished. Supplementing the basic seed diet for the caged bird as described above provides the total nutrition the bird needs to be healthy and live a long life.

Many fruits and vegetables are relished by canaries and can be offered in addition to your bird's daily diet.

DANGEROUS PLANTS

This is a listing of harmful plants that Leanne Bertino helped me compile. The poisonous part of the plant is listed in parentheses, as well as alternate names for the plants in question. This list is by no means inclusive of all harmful plants. When in doubt, keep your bird away from it.

Acocanthera (fruit and flowers)

Amaryllis (bulbs)

Amsinckia (also known as tarweed, foliage, seeds)

Anemone (wildflower - all parts)

Angel trumpet (flowers and leaves)

Apple (seeds)

Apricot (pits, inner seed)

Atropa autumn crocus (bulbs)

Avocado (foliage)

Azalea (leaves)

Spathiphyllum *hybrid.*

Balsam pear (seeds, outer rind of fruit)

Baneberry (berries, roots)

Common houseplant "dumb cane" or Dieffenbachia picta. *This is a highly toxic plant to all birds and should not be anywhere that the bird can reach.*

Beach pea (all parts)

Belladonna (all parts, especially black berries)

Betel nut palm (all parts)

Bird of paradise (seeds)

Bittersweet (berries)

Black locust (bark, sprouts, foliage)

Bleeding heart (foliage, roots)

Bloodroot (all parts)

Bluebonnet (all parts)

Blue-green algae (some forms are toxic)

Bottlebrush (flowers)

Boxwood (leaves, stems)

Buckeye horse chestnut (sprouts, nuts)

Buckthorn (fruit, bark)

Buttercup (sap, bulbs)

Calla lily (leaves)

Caladium (leaves)

Cardinal flower (all parts)

Carolina jessamine (foliage, flowers, sap)

Cassava (roots)

Castor bean (also castor oil-beans, leaves)

Chalice vine (aka trumpet vine - all parts)

Cherry tree (bark, twigs, leaves, pits)

Cherry laurel (foliage, flowers)

Chinaberry tree (berries)

Christmas berry (berries)

Christmas cactus (sap)

Christmas candle (sap)

Christmas rose (foliage, flowers)

Common privet (foliage, berries)

Coral plant (seeds)

Crocus (bulbs)

Croton (foliage, shoots)

Cyclamen (foliage, stems, flowers)

Daffodil (bulbs)

Daphne (berries)

Datura (berries)

Deadly amanita (all parts)

Deadly nightshade (all parts)

Death camas (all parts)

Death cap mushroom (all)

Dephinimum (all parts)

Deiffenbachia (aka dumbcane - leaves)

Dogwood (fruit),

Dutchman's breeches (foliage,roots)

Eggplant (all parts but fruit)

Elderberry (foliage)

Elephant's ear (aka taro - leaves, stem)

English ivy (berries, leaves)

Equisetum (all parts)

Euphorbia (aka spurges - foliage, flowers, sap)

False henbane (all parts)

Fiddleneck (aka senecio - all parts)

Fly agaric (aka amanita - all parts)

Four o'clock (all)

Foxglove (leaves, seeds)

Gelsemium (all)

Ghostweed (all)

Golden chain (aka laburnum - all parts, especially seeds)

Hemlock (all parts, especially roots and seeds)

Henvane (seeds), holly (berries)

Horse chestnut (nuts, twigs)

Thanksgiving cactus is beautiful to look at but toxic if ingested. Keep it out of your bird's reach.

Horsetail reed (aka equisetum (all)

Hyacinth (bulbs)

Hydrangea (flower bud)

Impatients (aka touch-me-not - all parts)

Indian turnip (aka jack-in-pulpit - all parts)

Iris (aka blue flag - bulbs)

Ivy (all forms - foliage, fruit)

Poison ivy proves toxic not only if ingested, but touched as well. The rash it can produce on a small canary would surely inflict death.

Jasmine (foliage, flowers, sap)

Jasmine star (foliage, flowers)

Jatropha (seeds, sap)

Java bean (aka lima bean - uncooked bean)

Jerusalem cherry (berries)

Jessamine (berries)

Jimsonweed (foliage, flowers, seed pods)

Johnson grass (all parts)

Juniper (needles, stems, berries)

Laburnum (all)

Lambkill (aka sheep laurel - all)

Lantana (immature berries)

Larkspur (all parts)

Laurel (all parts)

Lily of the valley (all parts including water in which they have been kept)

Lima bean (aka Java bean - (uncooked bean)

Lobelia (all parts)

Locoweed (all parts)

Lords and ladies (aka cuckoopint - all parts)

Lupine (foliage, pods, seeds)

Machineel (all), marijuana (leaves)

The sweetheart plant, Philodendron scandens, *has poisonous leaves and stem.*

Narcissus (bulbs)
Natal cherries (berries, foliage)
Nectarine (seeds, inner pit)
Nicotine bush (foliage, flowers)
Nightshades (all varieties - berries, leaves)
Oak (acorns, foliage)
Oleander (leaves, branches, nectar of blossoms)
Peach (pit)
Pear (seeds)
Pennyroyal (foliage, flowers)
Peony (foliage flowers)
Periwinkle (all)
Philodendron (leaves and stem)
Pikeweed (leaves, roots, immature berries)
Pine needles (berries)
Plum (foliage, inner seed)
Poinsettia (leaves, flowers)
Poison hemlock (foliage, seeds)
Poison ivy (sap)
Poison oak and poison sumac (foliage, fruit, sap)
Pokeweed (aka poke cherry - roots, fruit)

Mayapple - all parts, except fruit)
Mescal bean (seeds)
Milkweed (foliage)
Mistletoe (berries)
Moccasin flower (foliage, flowers)

Mock orange (fruit)
Monkshood (leaves, roots)
Morning glory (all parts)
Mountain laurel (leaves, shoots)
Mushrooms (most wild forms - caps, stems)

Hoya bella "rubra."

Friendship plant—**Pilea involucrata.**

Poppy (all parts)
Potato (eyes and new shoots)
Rivet (all parts, including berries)
Redwood (resinoids, leached wet wood)
Rhododendron (all parts)
Rhubarb (leaves)
Rosary peas (seeds - these seeds are illegally imported to make necklaces and rosaries)
Rosemary (foliage in some species)
Russian thistle (foliage, flowers)
Sage (foliage in some species)
Salmonberry (foliage, fruit)
Scarlet pimpernel (foliage, flowers, fruit),
Scotch broom (seeds),
Senecio (aka fiddleneck– all
Skunk cabbage (all parts)
Snapdragon (foliage, flowers)
Snowdrop (all parts especially buds)
Snow on the mountain (aka ghostweed - all parts)
Sweet pea (seeds and fruit)
Spanish bayonet (foliage, flowers)
Sudan grass (all)
Star of Bethlehem (foliage, flowers)
Sundew (foliage)
Sweet pea (seeds and fruit)
Tansy (foliage)

Too many houseplants that might prove safe if ingested look very much like those that are toxic. It is better to keep your pets away from all plants unless you are absolutely certain they are safe.

Weeping fig

Taro (aka elephant's ear (foliage)
Tiger lily (foliage, flowers, seed pods)
Toad lax (foliage)
Tobacco (leaves)
Tomato (foliage vines)
Touch-me-not (all)
Toyon berry (berries)
Trillium (foliage)
Trumpet vine (all)
Venus flytrap (all)
Verbena (foliage, flowers)
Virginia creeper (sap)
Wildflower (leaves, flower)
Wild parsnip (roots, foliage)
Wisteria (all parts)
Yam bean (roots, immature roots)
Yellow star thistle (foliage, flowers)
Yew (American, English and Japanese varieties - needles).

To keep the stress level of your canary to a minimum, it is best to establish a consistent routine and attempt to follow it each day.

such as fruits, vegetables or greens.

Every two weeks I suggest to thoroughly clean the cage by washing it in hot soapy water with a bit of bleach added (remove the perches before). Rinse well and leave to dry in the sun if possible. Replace the perches if they are clean; if not, replace them with clean ones. Perches can be cleaned with sandpaper or soaking in bleach water and allowing them to dry before using again. Seed cups should be washed and rinsed as well. Your pet canary can be placed in a small temporary cage while the large cage is being cleaned. To minimize trauma, the bird should be trained to enter the extra cage on its own. This is fairly simple. Move the two cages together with the cage doors open and facing each

Several times a week, allow your canary to bathe, making sure to do this early in the morning so that he has time to dry off.

GENERAL CARE

It is best to establish a consistent routine and attempt to follow it each day. In the morning, gently uncover the cage and talk or whistle beforehand so as not to startle the bird. Remove the water tube and replace it with a clean one filled with fresh, cool water. Remove the large seed cup, discarding the seeds in it and refill with fresh mix. Remove the treat cup, discard any remaining food in it (clean or replace if soiled) and refill. You can provide

some fruit or greens at this time. Remove dirty paper from the bottom of the cage. I stack about 10 to 12 layers of white paper towels every time I do a complete cage cleaning. Remove one layer at a time during each general cleaning, and only replace the toweling when all the sheets are used up. Several times a week allow the bird to bathe, making sure to do this early in the morning so that he has plenty of time to dry off. Throughout the day provide the bird with other treats other. Place a piece of greens in the spare cage to entice your bird in. Soon the canary will be hopping back and forth between the two cages. When it is time to do the scheduled cleanup, your bird will automatically enter the spare cage.

Your pet canary will eventually have to be handled to trim its nails. This is not difficult. If you feel uneasy doing this task, ask someone who is proficient to do it for you. Many bird stores or pet centers offer this task as a service to their customers or for a small fee. Your avian veterinarian can also do this for you.

Greens are very much enjoyed by canaries, and they are often used to lure birds into spare cages or bathing water.

When you give your canary's regular cage a thorough cleaning, it is best to transfer him to a smaller cage.

Health Issues

TYPICAL ILLNESSES AND RESPONSE

This is meant to be an overview of what might occur during your bird's lifetime. If you have a single canary and do not come into contact with other caged or wild birds, or their droppings, then you probably won't experience too many health-related problems. Keep in mind that many diseases are airborne, and you can bring in a wild bird's disease merely by stepping in its droppings.

Your pet canary's behavior will change should he become ill. He will not be as active and will eat less.

What does a bird look like when it is sick? Usually, its eyes will be smaller than normal and/or wet; they will lose their normal brightness. The nostrils may have a discharge. The bird will be fluffed up and listless. By the time this happens, the illness may be serious. Birds have learned not to show that they are sick as a defensive measure. As long as they do not appear sick they may not be preyed upon. So, when the bird demonstrates a sick appearance, it is really very, very sick, and immediate action should be taken.

Colds are fairly common and usually are cured with heat and rest. If the cold is persistent, oral medication and/or nebulization is prescribed.

Aspergillosis is a fungal infestation of the respiratory system generally caused by using old, moldy seed. This infection is usually fatal although some other types of fungal infections can be treated with nystatin.

Diarrhea can be treated with over-the-counter medicines available at your local pet store. Cheese and banana also help to bind the looseness. Diarrhea can be temporary or chronic. If it is the latter, perhaps an antibiotic is in order. When antibiotics are used, yogurt or cheese should be added to the diet to rebuild intestinal flora. Lactobacillus supplements that perform the same task are also available.

Mites can cause many problems. Red mites burrow under the skin, sucking the bird's blood supply. Baby birds can die if infested with these mites. Air sac mites infesting the air sacs can result in breathing difficulties manifested by wheezing and squeaking. Other mites can cause scaly legs and scaly face. If you suspect red mites, place a white cloth over the cage in the evening and then examine it the first thing in the morning. The mites will appear as small moving red dots, the red coming from the blood of the canary. Proper prevention can eliminate these things from happening. However, once they do, the best treatment is to use one drop of ivermictin rubbed into the back of the neck. Repeat this treatment in one week.

Feather lice will damage the feathers of the bird. Lice can be detected by holding up a feather to the light. Tracks where the lice have eaten the feathers are an indication that they are present. Regular spraying with a pyrethrin-based insecticide along with maintaining a clean cage and surroundings is the best deterrents.

There are other more serious diseases that require professional veterinary treatment and will usually not be encountered in the single-bird household.

Once you suspect that the bird is ill, separate it from any other birds you have to prevent spreading the disease and to keep the bird as calm as possible. Place your pet in a "hospital cage." If you don't have one, place a light bulb next to the cage. The extra warmth will help keep the body temperature from dropping and the bird can preserve its strength. Note the bird's condition and the condition of its droppings so that you can report these findings to a veterinarian or a more experienced person.

Becoming egg bound is a serious problem. It can be caused by improper diet, the egg breaking within the body and blocking passage of other eggs, or just due to the hen not being in optimal breeding condition. Heat (electric heat pad) is usually the cure,

Bathing is not a sign that your canary has mites. Your bird will act highly uncomfortable and will scratch a lot if he is infected with mites.

assisted by adding a few drops of warm olive oil to the oviduct and gently massaging the abdomen. If the shell is broken inside the bird it may cause peritonitis and the bird may die. Be very careful not to put too much pressure on the abdomen.

ACCIDENTS

Sometimes the strangest things can happen. Your canary can catch its toenail in the cage wires, it can bang its beak into the cage, catch its wing between the cage wires, or any number of other odd things. In any of these situations there may be a loss of blood and if you don't see this in time the bird may bleed to death. Always keep some styptic powder available. At other times, it may become frightened and actually faint. Most of the time they revive, and are none the worse for the wear.

OTHER PROBLEMS

There may be other situations that occur where the bird cannot be saved because it has passed the point of no return or the cure is not within our means. In such cases, euthanization is usually called for. Avian veterinarians have painless ways to perform this.

Mites and other parasites can be brought in from the wild on branches of outdoor trees or from visiting locations where infected birds live.

Breeding Equipment

I have been asked many times "What do I need to get started breeding?" "What size cages should be used?" "Should the cages be single or double breeders?" This section addresses the hardware items that a breeder of canaries will need, and also covers the setting up of these items in an efficient manner.

Let's start off with a breeding cage, which can be purchased or built. The degree of perfection is up to the individual. Canaries are capable of setting up house in the smallest and most unlikely of places. Many people have experienced success in breeding in a typical house cage, but in fairness to the breeding pair and their

Breeding cages that are made of wire are commonly used because they are easy to clean and sterilize.

offspring a larger cage is recommended. For most canaries a double breeder is recommended. This cage is usually of all wire construction and approximately 18 to 25 inches wide by 9 inches deep by 9 inches high. It comes with both solid and wire partitions that slide into the center of the cage. These dividers are useful in initially separating and introducing the male and female to each other; and then separating the male from the hen and/or the young from the hen as she sets up for the following brood. The cage should have four perches at mid-height level. Some have a long perch running across the bottom to allow the birds to access feed and water cups.

Canaries are capable of setting up house in the smallest and most unlikely of places; however, a double breeder offers the most room for the birds and proves very successful.

Single breeding cages are also available, but I find them to be rather restrictive, whereas a triple breeder provides even more flexibility. Some vendors supply cage fronts, allowing you to build your own cage with dimensions at least as large as the dimensions of the fronts. Wood is preferable to metal because it can be worked easily—even by the amateur. One suggestion for those building their own cages with either prefabricated cage fronts or welded wire fabric: make one long cage with multiple fronts. Divide it with slide-in partitions for breeding, and then use it as a flight cage later on. Drawers come in handy for cleaning, for placing items on the floor, and for picking up baby birds and other items that have fallen on the floor. There are commercial breeding cage systems available that incorporate these features. A word of caution when using wooden cages: paint with a lead free paint (most are nowadays) and allow the paint to dry thoroughly before introducing birds into them.

There are many accessories for the breeding cage, some of which are fairly obvious. Feeders and drinkers are the first. Some cages come equipped with brackets and/or features to accommodate them. Some cage fronts do not, so feeders that will hang or mount sturdily in order for the birds to feed at ease are recommended. The most popular drinkers are tube drinkers that have a vertical glass or plastic tube. This tube fits into a plastic base that slides in between the wires into the cage. The tube stays on the outside, making changing of the water an easy task.

There is another type of drinker that is popular. It is the kind with a narrow metal tube running down from a bottle-shaped container. The narrow tube contains one or two balls. One of the balls is partially exposed at the open end. The bird pushes on the ball with its beak and a drop of water comes out. The advantage of this kind of water dispenser is that the water does not easily become

As one becomes an experienced canary breeder, it becomes easier to know what accessories prove most successful and what methods are most reliable.

contaminated. However, the balls in the tube of this type of drinker may stick and prevent water flows so your constant attention to this possibility is strongly recommended.

Another type of drinker that is useful, especially in flight cages, sits on the floor and allows several birds to drink simultaneously. Automated watering systems are also available, but are costly and mostly used by large-scale breeders.

There is a multitude of feeder designs; use the ones best suited to your needs. I

Aggressiveness or fighting sometimes occurs among birds when there is not enough food available or too little space. Always be certain to provide ample amounts of these for success.

When more than one bird is housed in a cage it is important to have feeders or drinkers that are easily accessible.

recommend that you have a double set of feeders and drinkers so that one set can be soaked in a bleach solution while the others are in use.

Nest pans are typically used for canary breeding. They are available in both metal and plastic. Plastic nests are preferred because they don't rust and are easy to clean. Both come with hooks or clips to mount on the cage wires. Some need to be adapted for mounting to a solid surface.

Breeders encountering this situation have attached (by welding or soldering) bent welding wire to metal pans. The bent wire is then passed through eyehooks screwed into the cage wall. Felt pads are used to line the nest pan and can be attached by sewing or using carpet tape. Burlap strands (which have been washed, sterilized, rinsed, and dried) are used as nesting materials. These materials can be attached to the cage front with a

A variety of nest pans are available from your local pet store. Be certain that the one you choose is easy to clean and sterilize.

Tools are available from your local pet store to assist you in putting on your canary's band.

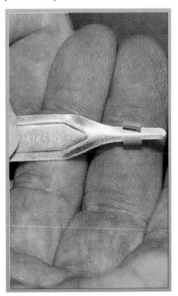

clothespin or placed into a hopper arrangement.

Other useful items are artificial eggs, leg bands, band cutters, a candling light, and cuttlebone. Canary breeders utilize artificial eggs to ensure that all eggs hatch at the same time. The first three eggs are removed and replaced with the artificial ones each morning. On the fourth morning the artificial eggs are removed and replaced with the real eggs. Closed leg bands are applied just before the feet get too big to be able to put them on without hurting the bird—for canaries it is on the sixth day. Sometimes a lubricant helps to slide the band on.

A good band cutter is an absolute necessity in the bird room, usually to remove a band when the leg has become swollen or infected. Band cutters that are adequate for the pet owner or a breeder are available from local pet stores.

Candling lights allow the determination of fertility without removing the eggs from the nest. Again, your local bird stores sell lights that allow candling of the eggs while they are still in the nest. A makeshift candler can be made by placing a collar or sleeve around the bulb end of a flashlight. A hole large enough for the egg to fit partially in the hole is cut into the cover which is taped to the sleeve. The light is turned on and the egg placed into the hole allowing the contents of the egg to be viewed.

Proper lighting is essential to successful canary breeding. Artificial light is almost always necessary in an indoor breeding situation.

Cuttlebone is necessary and provides a source of calcium and other minerals. Mineral supplements, also essential for egg formation, should be provided on a regular basis. Your pet canary should be allowed to bathe regularly.

Regular spraying with a pyrethrin-based insecticide is a necessity. Other first aid items such as ivermictin, and antibiotics (oral and topical) are also suggested, along with a hospital cage.

I recommend that all equipment in a birdroom be as standardized as possible. This simplifies the daily tasks and reduces the overall time required for routine maintenance. Another suggestion is to use full spectrum bulbs to help ensure fertility. Lights should be on a timer to provide a gradual ramp up (number of "daylight" hours) to breeding startup and a consistent lighting pattern during breeding season. A night-light is helpful in that it will help the hen find her way back to the nest should she

leave it for any reason during the lights out period. I also find that a small cart on wheels is very helpful as is a hospital cage and several spare cages.

The most important lesson that I learned in my many years of breeding is to maintain consistency in the birdroom. If cages, feeders, drinkers, and other equipment are all the same, chore time is significantly reduced. This applies to breeders of all types of birds. Standardization helps

Proper food, lighting and exercise all contribute to the good health and success of your breeding program.

to make your birdroom activities more pleasurable and enables you to spend more time actually enjoying the birds. Another lesson is to prepare well in advance of the breeding season. All of the contents of the room should be removed and the room thoroughly scrubbed down with a disinfectant. All of the cages should be washed similarly. Cages need to be repaired and repainted if necessary. Then all the equipment is reinstalled and the birds introduced.

I am sure that there are plenty of other hints and suggestions that will be helpful to you. I have tried to list the ones that I feel are most important to help you succeed in your breeding program.

PREPPING THE BIRDS

Lighting Requirements
Scientific studies have shown that light is the single most important influence on the birds' breeding condition. As the length of daylight increases from wintertime's 9 hours up to 12 and 14 hours, certain factors are triggered to advance them to the breeding state. Males will begin to sing lustily. The female abdomen swells and the oviduct becomes larger; hens start picking up nesting materials, holding these things at the back of their beaks. Because most breeders maintain their flocks indoors, artificial light is used to substitute for sunlight. Full spectrum lights mimic the sun and enhance optimum fertility. Many fluorescent tubes and incandescent bulbs that simulate full-spectrum light are available from fine stores everywhere.

Kevin Gorman produced the following chart to guide the breeder into, through, and out of the canary-breeding season (you can adjust to your own cycle by moving the dates up or down on the chart):

Part of this chart shows time changes in bi-weekly increments. Spread the time changes over the 14 days between major changes. The gradual day-to-day changes will allow the birds to become accustomed to the adjustments more comfortably.

Special Diet

During the molt, a complete diet of seeds, egg food (sometimes called nestling food), and vegetation should be supplied as the birds will require both protein and fat to replace the feathers they have lost. A "quiet" period, noted by the diminishing daylight hours, follows the molt allowing the birds to recover from the previous breeding season. Color enhancers (e.g., beta carotene, and canthaxanthin), if desired, are added to both the nestling food and drinking water until the molt is complete. Egg food and oily seeds should be virtually curtailed so that the birds do not become fat. The egg food is then gradually increased as the ensuing breeding season approaches.

DATE	LIGHTS ON	LIGHTS OFF	ACTIVITIES
Jan. 01	7:30 am	4:30 PM	Active and singing
Jan. 07	7:30 am	4:45 PM	
Jan. 14	7:15 am	5:00 PM	
Jan. 21	7:00 am	6:00 PM	
Feb. 07	6:15 am	7:00 PM	
Feb. 14	6:00 am	7:00 PM	Males should be vigorously singing. Hens will be extremely active carrying shreds of newspapers and flying only part of the distance across the cage before turning.
Mar. 07	Put males and females together.		Should begin nesting within 1 week
May 01	5:30 am	7:00 PM	Second nest of young started.
May 15	5:30 am	7:15 PM	
Jun 01	5:00 am	7:30 PM	Put all hens in flight unless they are still feeding. Last nest of young.
Jun 15	5:15 am	7:45 PM	Adults start moulting.
July 01	5:00 am	8:00 PM	Adults rather inactive, males not singing, first nest young begin molting.
July 15	5:15 am	7:45 PM	
Aug. 01	5:30 am	7:30 PM	Second nest of young begins molting.
Aug. 15	5:45 am	7:15 PM	
Sep. 01	6:00 am	6:45 PM	Young males starting to sing
Sep. 15	6:15 am	6:30 PM	
Oct. 01	6:30 am	5:00 PM	Adult birds become more active.
Oct. 15	6:45 am	5:45 PM	
Nov. 01	7:00 am	5:15 PM	
Nov. 15	7:00 am	4:45 PM	
Dec. 01	7:00 am	4:15 PM	All birds fully active.
Dec. 15	7:15 am	4:15 PM	

Because the hens are inactive when incubating the eggs, egg food should not be offered until a few days before hatching begins. The young will not need to be fed immediately after they emerge, as the egg sac will provide them with enough nutrition for a day or so. The quantity of egg food supplied should be consumed within two to three hours. This, along with placing the food in a shallow dish, will help prevent spoilage. Greens are not supplied the first week. A variety of seeds should be available at all times. Soaked seed is an excellent supplement and can be fed in a separate dish or mixed in with the nestling food. The same holds true for sprouted seed and grated carrot. This regimen should be followed as the young are weaned and separated.

Preparation of Nestling Food

Nestling or egg food is a nutritious, high protein food complete with vitamins and minerals. Today there are many sources of quality nestling foods available. If you prefer, you can make your own. The following generic formula will produce approximately 2.5 pounds of dry nestling food mix: 1 lb. dried bread crumbs, $1^{1}/_{2}$ lb. soybean meal, $^{1}/_{4}$ lb. wheat germ meal, $^{1}/_{2}$ lb. oatmeal, $^{1}/_{4}$ lb. corn meal, 1 oz. alfalfa, 4 grams cultured yeast, 1 teaspoon calcium phosphate, 1 teaspoon kelp, 1 teaspoon salt, 1 teaspoon gelatin, 1 oz. sunflower meal, 1 teaspoon dextrose, 1 teaspoon complete mineral mix, 5 grams complete multiple vitamin (amounts of minerals and vitamins depends on their respective formulations), 1 oz. poppy seed, 5 grams beta carotene (canthaxanthin can be added for red birds). Just prior to feeding, grate 1 hard cooked egg and add it to 1 heaping tablespoon of the dry mix formula; mix thoroughly. Grated carrot or soaked seed can also be added. Feed only enough that can be consumed in two to three hours. Refrigerate any unused portion for two days, and then discard.

Young canaries do not need to be fed by their parents immediately after they emerge from the egg; however, this soon changes and they gape wide to be fed from their parents.

Other Considerations

Because the nestling food is very rich, occasionally a feeding parent may suffer intestinal distress. A pinch of Epsom salts in the drinking water usually relieves this problem. Sometimes a parent will stop feeding as well. This could be the result of the intestinal distress or just plain boredom with the same food being provided over and over again. This is why a variety of foods should be provided. Another solution is allowing the parent to bathe.

SEXING PRIOR TO BREEDING

To have a successful breeding season it is necessary to have the birds come into full breeding condition before "setting them up." When this happens the birds will be eager to mate and fighting will be virtually eliminated. As noted earlier, the males will be singing lustily and their vents will increase in length and be in a somewhat ninety-degree position relative to their abdomens. The hens will tear

Above: *Red-factor canaries must be fed special food to enhance their red color.*

Left: *New foodstuffs should not be given to breeding canaries unless they seem bored with their present diet or are not properly feeding their young.*

41

The average female canary in breeding condition lays between four to six eggs.

up paper and carry these shreds and other possible nesting materials in the farthest part of the beak. Their bottoms will swell, becoming pear shaped and be void of feathers. The vent opening will become much larger. Remember that it is essential for both cock and hen to be completely ready for breeding before pairing can begin.

SETTING UP PAIRS AND SEQUENCE OF EVENTS

When the hens appear to be ready, remove them from the flight cage and place them into the breeding cages (one hen for each breeding cage) that have been cleaned and prepared with the proper equipment noted earlier. After allowing a few days for them to become accustomed to the new surroundings, place a nest pan into the cage. A liner pad should be bonded or attached in some way to the pan to prevent the liner from being pulled out. The bottom of the liner should have been dusted with pyrethrin powder before placing it into the pan.

This will prevent insect infestation of the nest. Add nesting material to the cage. It can be attached with a clip or clothespin, or placed into a hopper attached to the cage. The male is placed in one-half of the cage after a solid divider has divided it. The pair

When the canary eggs hatch, the parent birds will toss the shells out of the nest or eat them.

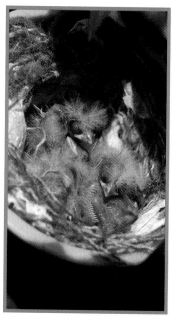

will call to each other and after a few days the solid divider is removed and replaced with a wire divider. By this time the hen should have started to build the nest. Once the male has been seen to feed the hen through the divider wires, the divider can be removed.

Squatting low on a perch in response to the male's singing the hen will allow the cock to mount her. Copulation being completed, laying eggs should commence in a few days. Usually, four to six eggs are laid at a rate of one egg per day. Eggs are laid the first thing in the morning. It is common practice to replace the first three eggs with artificial eggs. The removed eggs are placed in a small container lined with sterile cotton, tissue or birdseed, turning the eggs each day. On the fourth day the artificial eggs are removed and the hen's eggs returned to the nest. Since hatchlings grow at an amazing rate, this procedure assures that the first four eggs will hatch on the same day and there will be equal competition to be fed by the parents. If this was not done, the chick hatched on the first day would have a distinct advantage over a chick hatched on the fourth day.

On the day before as well as two days before scheduled hatching, the hen should be allowed to bathe and/or the eggs be sprayed lightly with warm water. This helps the chick break out of the shell. Also begin to supply small amounts of egg food to the pair.

When the eggs hatch, the parents will toss the shells

out of the nest or eat them. Begin feeding a generous amount of egg food. Remember not to feed any greens during the chicks' first three days. It will be necessary to increase the amount of egg food each day as chicks will require more and more food as they grow. Feed only enough that can be consumed in two to three hours. A shallow dish is preferable because it allows any left over food to dry before it begins to spoil. If possible, provide egg food three times per day, in the morning, in the early afternoon, and later in the evening. Remove the egg food just prior to the lights being turned off. The lights should be dimmed gradually if possible, and a night-light kept on the entire night. If your schedule does not permit a three times per day feeding schedule, feed first thing in the morning and at dinner time.

FLEDGLINGS AND THE SECOND BROOD

The young will emerge from the nest at about two weeks of age and can be weaned three weeks later. Most likely the hen will begin a second clutch after the chicks have left the nest and they will have to be removed once she starts laying eggs. Not removing the first brood increases the possibility of the chicks breaking the newly laid eggs. If this is a problem and the chicks have not been completely weaned, the young can be separated from the hen by installing a wire divider, and placing them on the other side of it with or without the male. Chicks still begging for food can be fed

The young canaries will begin their first molt at about 12 to 14 weeks of age. They will lose all their feathers except their flight feathers and are sometimes referred to as unflighted.

through the divider wires and they can be placed in a small flight once they are fully weaned. As they get bigger and stronger they can be placed in a larger flight. The chicks will begin their first molt in about 12 to 14 weeks of age. They will lose all their feathers except the flight feathers. This is why they are sometimes referred to as "unflighted" birds.

CONCLUSION OF BREEDING SEASON

The adults will begin to molt when they complete their breeding activities. The molt takes approximately 12 to 14 weeks to complete. Placing all the birds in large flights will prepare them for the following breeding season. Birds that are expected to compete in bird shows should be trained in smaller cages.

Young canaries must be removed from the breeding cage as soon as the hen begins to lay her second clutch of eggs.

Bird Shows and Exhibitions

WHAT IS YOUR ROLE?

Most bird clubs sponsor a show or exhibition on an annual basis. Canary shows are usually held from mid-September until the end of December. This is the place to bring your bird to be judged so that you can determine your success as a breeder. Type and colorbred canaries are judged according to standards developed by the specialty organization for each breed. More recently these canaries have been judged using a point system with 100 being the perfect score. At some shows you may still see type and colorbred being judged by comparison.

Each kind of song canary is judged somewhat differently than the other. Basically, they are all being judged on the quality of their songs. Standards have been set for singers too.

A candidate has to serve an apprenticeship and successfully pass a battery of tests to become a judge. Each specialty club will certify judges that meet its requirements. For example, I am certified as a colorbred canary Judge by both the National Colorbred Association (NCA) and the COM-USA.

If you don't choose to be an exhibitor you may want to assist other club members in running the show itself. Many workers are needed to successfully plan and run a show. Some of the "jobs" are organizing or dealing with catalogs, advertising, food and beverage sales, and assisting judges as stewards and secretaries.

If you intend to exhibit your canaries at a bird show you should begin preparations in August. Breeding season is well over with for canaries by then and the adults should be completing their molt. The youngsters should be fully

A canary bird show is where you can bring your bird to be judged so that you can determine your success as a breeder.

44

fledged as well. It is the opportune time to start doing a thorough cleanup of the bird room, and selecting birds that will be retained for future breeding and/or exhibitions and those that will be disposed of. This section deals with what is necessary to prepare for bird shows and exhibitions.

When you arrive at the bird show with your birds, they will be exposed to conditions quite unlike the security of the environment where they were bred and raised. First, they will be placed in a very small show cage that will then be put into some type of carrier that holds more than one show cage. This is usually a closed container made either of rigid (wood, screening) or flexible (vinyl, canvas) materials. Now in a somewhat darkened environment they will be carried about by their owners and transported by various means to the show hall where the show cages will be unceremoniously removed, tagged, and placed on tables waiting to be classified. At this time the show secretaries will enter the birds into the official show book. The cages will then be handled many, many times by a variety of people, none of whom will be familiar. There will be plenty of noise as well and a lot of commotion. The birds may be fortuitous enough to arrive the evening before judging which will enable them to get a good night's rest and help them become acclimated to the new surroundings. Or they may have the misfortune of being brought in the

Your very best canaries should be selected from your stock, not only for showing, but to be retained for breeding.

Canaries can be hand tamed but it takes a lot of time and patience.

morning of the show and their discomfort will certainly be evident during the judging.

I will pay particular attention to colorbred and type canaries but at the same time mention that there are also categories for judging the songsters like Rollers, Waterslagers, American Singers, and Spanish Timbrados. Colorbred canaries and some type canaries (e.g., Glosters) are judged in box type cages with wire fronts while other type Canaries (e.g., Borders, Yorkshires) are judged in all-wire cages. Sometimes canaries are judged by a point system and at other times they are judged by comparison and elimination. The choice is dependent on the sponsoring club and the method that the judge prefers to use (usually sanctioned by a national or specialty club).

Prior to judging, the stewards of a particular division will certify that the bird has been categorized and placed in the proper "class." If not, corrections will be made and the secretary advised. Prior to judging, the birds are usually placed on long tables, that are perpendicular to the judging stand. The stewards bring the birds up to the judging stand where the judge will score the birds by points or comparison and relay the results to the secretary. The birds are judged first by class, then by section, and then finally by division. Birds not in the running are returned to the tables while those that may have winning potential are kept on or close to the judging stand. As a finale, the top winners of a division are placed on the judging stand for all to see. Depending on the length of the show, awards may be given out immediately after the judging is finished, later that evening, or even on the next day. Also dependent on how long the show runs, is when the birds can be removed. In a one-day event, birds can be removed at the end of judging. Sometimes, birds from the local area are required to stay longer and out-of-town birds are allowed to leave earlier. In any of these situations, the exhibitor is required to have his/her birds checked out by a representative of the show committee. Returning the birds home results in even more stress than leaving because the birds are extremely tired from the judging event.

I will attempt to provide some helpful hints for preparing your birds for a competitive bird show. First of all, and probably most important, they should become accustomed to the show cage. I recommend keeping a set of cages for training and a set for the show. This will provide a clean cage for show day. The easiest way to help a bird lose its initial fear of a show cage is to mount the show cage on

Canaries are judged first by class, then by section, and finally by division.

As a finale to the canary show, the top winners of a division are placed on the judging stand for all to see.

to the flight or breeder cage that the bird is housed in. Some song food, greens or other treats will entice it to enter the cage. Once the first bird goes in others will follow, and will enter and leave as they please. This can be done at any time, the earlier the better.

As show time approaches, the selected birds are allowed to enter the show cage that is closed and removed from the larger cage. The bird is kept in the show cage for several hours and then allowed to return to its conventional cage. Gradually increase the length of time the bird spends

in the cage until about five days before the show; the bird should not be removed from the show cage. During this time period you will have many birds in many show cages. Each day try to move the cages around, placing them in different locations, and holding them close to bright lights. You can also tap lightly on the cage with a perch or pen. It is also helpful for others to do the same things so that the birds get used to strangers. The last suggestions will help your bird become used to the actions that stewards and judges will use at the show. After each one of these practice sessions, provide the bird with a little treat. Soon you will see that it will be at ease in the cage and actually look forward to the training sessions. About a week before the show, check the beak and the toenails and trim them if necessary. Some exhibitors will shampoo their birds about seven to ten days before the show. Whether you do this or not is up to you; I highly recommend this for white birds, as they must be absolutely clean white. Also, make sure that the feet are clean. Another trick that can be used is to spray the bird with a solution of glycerin and water. To make this solution, dissolve 1 drop of glycerin in a quart of boiling water, mix thoroughly and allow to cool to room temperature. Spray the bird with the cooled solution on a daily basis. Start at seven days before the show and stop on the day before the show. Do not spray on the day of the show.

Transfer the bird into the show cage that it will be

Your show canary will spend much time inside a small show cage and he must be trained to withstand such accommodations.

It is highly recommended that you shampoo a white bird at least a week prior to a show because he should be absolutely clean white.

the show. I have seen birds almost die because they didn't recognize the water drinker. Lastly, most canary divisions require a mixture of canary and canola seed on the floor of the cage. Use common sense in adding the seed mix. The layer of seeds should be high enough to completely cover the floor, yet not too deep. Another caution: do not use a colored (vitamized) seed mix. Some judges may consider this as "marking" the cage and could disqualify the entry as they would if the cage had other markings on it such as tape or thumb tacks. Most canary divisions utilize standardized cages for each division. The colorbred canary associations have adopted one standard cage which will be mandatory at the 2000 National Cage Bird Show.

Wash your canary's feet and claws and clip the toenails prior to the show if necessary.

By following these suggestions, you will be assured of a less stressed bird, which "shows" much better. Training and cleanliness are extremely important.

exhibited in. Before doing this, check for any loose or broken feathers and pull them out. By doing this they will lose less points then by having a defective feather showing and, hopefully, the judge may not notice the missing feather. Make sure that the perches are clean, secure (don't wobble), and of the correct diameter. The perches should also be scored lengthwise to provide a firm gripping surface. Untrained birds and birds that are unable to "pose" correctly because of slipping on the perch can be the difference between winning and losing. Lastly, provide the bird with a drinker of fresh water; please note that the water container used in training should be the same type as the one used in

Show cages must all be of the same color, type, and are not permitted to be "marked" in any way.

Guide to Canaries

COLORBRED CANARIES

Canaries can be classified into three separate categories, namely colorbred, type, and song. I begin this section with a discussion of colorbred canaries.

Colorbred canaries are bred for their coloring. Lipochrome, melanin, classic color, yellow, white, red, ivory, mosaic, opal, pastel, green, blue, bronze, silver, ino, isabel, recessive, sex-linked, agate, and gold are some of the names that are used to identify them. And in many cases combinations of these names are utilized. Do most or some of these names confuse you? Well if they do, you are not alone. Trying to come to grips with them, especially for the beginner, can be extremely difficult. To further confuse the issue, an entirely different set of names is used to identify the coloration and feather characteristics of type canaries.

There are approximately 50 different colors of canaries as classified by specialty club organizations. Combinations of these colors further increase the number of different possibilities. It is no wonder that there is confusion when we try to comprehend and discuss intelligently the multitude of canary colors.

To help you understand better, let's go back to the very beginning when the only canaries that existed

were the wild birds that inhabited the Canary and the Madeira Islands (Fig. 1). These birds had a dull green coloration and were not very spectacular in appearance. The males, however, did possess an attractive song,

attractive enough for Spanish sailors stopping at these ports to trap them and take them home. The first recorded instance of this is 1478. Some canaries were taken to Germany but only males were sold for fear that

This is a yellow variegated green Yorkshire canary.

their corner on the market might be lost. Around 1650, one of the ships became wrecked and the birds were blown by the winds to the island of Elba. There a new strain showing more yellow than the original Canary Island strain developed. Eventually these birds were taken to Italy and on to Germany. These were the beginnings of all the colorbred and type canaries that exist today. Incidentally, the birds were named after the islands and not vice versa.

Only green canaries were recorded in 1677. By the year 1713 three color varieties were known: green, yellow and "blond," and in 1766 a tremendous jump to 29 varieties was recorded.

Canaries come in three basic ground colors: yellow, white and red (or red-orange) with yellow being the original ground color of the wild bird. There are two varieties of white, dominant white and recessive white.

There are also melanin pigments. Lipochrome and melanin names are detailed in Figure 2.

The melanin pigments are phaeomelanin brown, eumelanin black, and eumelanin brown. Phaeomelanin brown is located on the edges of the feathers while the eumelanin pigments are "located on each side of the center shaft of the feather and throughout the lower third of the feather," as quoted by Geoff Walker in *Coloured, Type and Song Canaries: A Complete Guide* (Blanford Press, 1987).

As a generalization, and please keep in mind that this

Figure 2 GROUND COLORS AND PIGMENTS OF CANARIES

GROUND COLORS	PIGMENTS
Yellow	Phaeomelanin Brown
White (2 kinds)	Eumelanin Brown
Red (since 1926)	Eumelanin Black

Yellow Frosted canary.

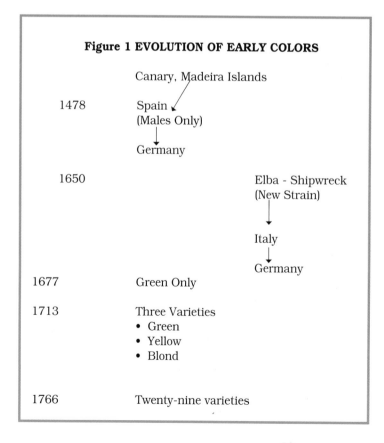

Figure 1 EVOLUTION OF EARLY COLORS

Canary, Madeira Islands

1478   Spain
        (Males Only)

        Germany

1650   Elba - Shipwreck
                                        (New Strain)

                                        Italy

                                        Germany

1677   Green Only

1713   Three Varieties
        • Green
        • Yellow
        • Blond

1766   Twenty-nine varieties

This is an example of a variegated Scot Fancy.

is very general, canaries that do not have any pigmentation are referred to as lipochrome canaries and those that do as melanin (or melanic) canaries. Lipochrome birds with absolutely no pigment are called "clear" while those that have areas of melanic pigmentation are called "variegated" and the pattern is called variegation. Melanin birds that have no pigmentation only in flight and/or tail feathers are referred to as "foul." If other areas have no pigment then the bird is also called "variegated." A "heavy variegated" bird is one which has a proportionately large area(s) of pigmentation. A canary is "lightly variegated" if it has small areas of pigmentation and "ticked" for even smaller areas.

Combinations of lipochrome ground colors and melanic pigment result in a number of different colored birds.

Combinations of lipochrome ground colors and melanic pigments result in a number of different colors as shown in Figure 3. For instance a yellow ground bird with black and brown pigments is a "green;" with only black it is a "gold agate;" with only brown it is called a "gold brown;" and with only diluted brown it is a "gold isabel." "Isabel" in the old days was referred to as

51

"dilute," "bronze" was "mahogany," "red-orange brown" was "copper," and "silver brown" was "fawn." Looking at Figure 3, note that all the colors under the melanin heading are referred to as "classic colors." There are other mutations which will be covered later.

Let's briefly return to the lipochromes. I stated earlier that there were two kinds of white, dominant white and recessive white. These terms have to do with how those colors are transmitted from the parents to the offspring.

Figure 3 LIPOCHROME AND MELANIN COLORS

Ground Color	No Pigment	Black & Brown	Black Only	Brown Only	Diluted Brown
Yellow	Yellow Lipochrome	Green	Gold Agate	Gold Brown	Gold Isabel
White	White Lipochrome	Blue	Silver Agate	Silver Brown	Silver Isabel
Red	Red Orange Lipochrome	Bronze	Red Orange Agate	Red Orange Brown	Red Orange Isabel

A good example of a clear, yellow lipochrome bird compared to a variegated or melanic one.

Dominant white birds are just that—white, with some yellow or red on the edges of the flight feathers. Recessive white birds are completely white, devoid of any ground color in the feathers and have a slight difference in skin color. Red (actually red-orange) canaries, unlike the white, are not a natural mutation. They originated from canaries crossed with the Black-hooded Venezuelan Siskin. Canaries possessing the red color factor were, and sometimes still, called Red-factor canaries. Numerous articles have been written about this subject and many of these can be obtained by checking back issues of hobbyist magazines.

The primary modes of inheritance are homozygous and heterozygous dominant, homozygous recessive, and sex-linked recessive. For simplicity sakes I will refer to these as dominant, recessive, and sex-linked, respectively. Basically, in dominant birds what you see is what you get. A yellow mated to a dominant white will produce both yellow and white offspring, one half of each color. With the recessive trait, both parents must either show or carry the mutated gene. With sex-linked inherit-ance, the mutated gene must be either seen or carried by the male or seen on the female to be transmitted to the youngsters.

The different color mutations categorized by mode of inheritance are listed in Figure 4. It also lists the dates that they were first reported. Please note that what may have appeared to be the current agate was first reported in the year 1700 but the mutation probably disappeared and didn't reappear until 1900.

The Black-hooded Siskin was originally crossed with the canary and has since been known to be responsible for the red coloring in the red-factor canary.

Figure 4 MUTATIONS
LISTED BY INHERITANCE MODES AND DATE OF FIRST RECORDING

Dominant Homozygous/ Heterozygous	Homozygous Recessive	Sex Linked Recessive
(Intensive/Non-Intensive)*		Brown (1750) Agate (~1700, 1900) Isabel (~1700, 1900)
Dominant White (1920)	Recessive White (1908) Opal (1949)	
		Ivory (1950)
	Satinette (1960) Ino (1967)	(Mosaic [Old])* Pastel (1960)

* Note: Intensive/Non-Intensive and Mosaic are feather types; not colors as the others.

There are other factors that influence color. These are due to feather type (Fig. 4) and are currently referred to as intensive, non-intensive, and mosaic (formerly called non-frost, frost and dimorphic, respectively). Intensive and non-intensive are equivalent to yellow and buff, terms used by type canary enthusiasts. Basically the non-intensive feather is broader and has a white frosting along its outer edge. The mosaics have a much broader feather that has even less lipochrome than the frost. Mosaic canaries lack color throughout the body with the exception of the areas around the eyes, wing butts and rump where the ground color almost appears to be amplified. Two types of mosaic exist, the classic or old mosaic that is sex-linked and the new type mosaic.

Now, I will review additional information about the other mutations (Fig. 3). All of the melanin mutations basically change the original black/brown pigmentation in one way or another. The brown mutation changes black to a deep brown with a medium gray underflue. The horny

A white canary cannot be bred with another white bird. This causes a lethal gene and the chicks either die before hatching or shortly thereafter.

(i.e., the beak and legs) areas are flesh colored (as compared to black/brown [green, blue, bronze] which have black horny areas). The isabel factor further reduces the brown. The agate factor modifies all of the melanin pigments. It eliminates the brown and leaves the black behind. The underflue is dark gray and horny areas are flesh-colored. Agate birds exhibit very noticeable dark streaks on the side of their heads. These are referred to as the mustache.

Birds exhibiting the ivory factor appear to have a film (like a soap film) over their plumage. Typical nomenclature is yellow ivory for yellow birds, white ivory for white, and rose ivory for red ground birds. Some Europeans refer to lipochrome ivory birds as pastels, however, this causes considerable confusion since we, in the states, use the term "pastel" to describe a melanic dilution.

The red-factor canary is not a natural mutation; it originated from canaries crossed with the Black-hooded Siskin.

The pastel factor further dilutes brown pigment to a point where the brown is no longer visible on an isabel and the bird appears to be a lipochrome. However, microscopic examination shows that the brown pigment is not entirely eliminated. "Graywings" are black-brown pastels that show distinct gray striations on the flights of unflighted (first year) birds. These striations become less noticeable after the first year.

In the opal canary, the black eumelanin is changed to dark silver and all of the brown disappears. The underflue is dark silver to charcoal. This results in a completely different looking coloration. The satinette factor is a further mutation of agates and isabels, which totally inhibits eumelanin black and phaeomelanin brown, leaving the eumelanin brown unchanged. These birds have very bright red eyes and a dark beige underflue. The satinette mutation of an isabel canary has brown striations on its back while the same mutation on an agate provides a bird that appears to be a lipochrome.

The ino mutation replaces eumelanin pigments with white leaving a white spangle effect. The eyes are also bright red like the satinette and the underflue is a pale beige. Two fairly recent mutations are the topaz and the onyx. Standards for these mutations have not been established.

Earlier I mentioned the four modes of inheritance—homozygous dominant, heterozygous dominant, recessive, and sex-linked. It is at this point that things get complicated. The terms and formulas used in describing genetics and formulas can be intimidating. To prevent this, I will give examples of what is produced in each mode of inheritance without referring to "X's," "Y's" and "Z's." Then by substituting different mutations within each mode, offspring for other pairings can be predicted. Those seriously interested in learning more about genetics can do this on their own (e.g., by visiting the library's genetics' section or joining a bird club).

Figure 5 illustrates what the offspring of a dominant white and yellow canary pairing will be. This holds true for either lipochrome or melanin birds. The chart can also be used to predict the outcome of intensive/non-intensive pairings (by substituting non-intensive for normal yellow and intensive for dominant white) and clear/self/variegated pairings (by substituting variegated for dominant white and self for normal yellow and clear for homozygous dominant white).

Figure 6 shows the offspring of the pairing of recessive canaries, in this

A silver agate opal canary. In the opal canary, the black eumelanin is changed to dark silver and all of the brown disappears.

case the opal. Recessive white and ino can be substituted for opal to determine the outcome of these respective pairings.

The results of pairing the sex-linked ivory mutation are depicted in Figure 7. Other mutations that can be predicted from this chart are brown, agate, isabel, pastel, satinette, and old type mosaic.

It is important to note that any one bird may have many different mutated factors as in "red agate opal ivory" or "gold isabel pastel."

It is extremely helpful to see actual specimens to reinforce the above learning. I suggest visiting breeders and their bird rooms, attending shows, joining local and national color bred canary specialty clubs (e.g. National Color Bred Association [NCA], and C.O.M.-USA, Inc.), reading magazines and books.

Possibly the most popular type canary among the general population is the Gloster. This bird is affectionately referred to as the "bird with the Beatles haircut."

TYPE CANARIES

While some breeders were trying to achieve excellence in the birds' song style or coloration, others were attempting to change the bodily or "type" configurations to their own specifications. The section on color bred canaries provides a brief history of the evolution of the wild canary to the colors that are available today. Some of the original birds bred for color are now considered as type canaries. Examples of these are the lizard and crested canaries. It is extremely interesting to trace the evolution of the different types. The intent of this section is to expose the reader to what the different type canaries look like and what some of their identifiable characteristics are.

A very interesting variety of canary is the frill. Pictured here is a Northern Dutch Frill. Notice the feathers coming out and curling back all around the body.

**Figure 5 DOMINANT HETEROZYGOUS
PAIRING RESULTS**

Dominant White, M or F
+ Normal Yellow, M or F
50% Dominant White
50% Normal Yellow

Dominant White + Dominant White
25% Normal yellow
50% Dominant White
25% Dominant White (Homozygous)

Normal Yellow + Normal Yellow
100% Normal Yellow

**Figure 7 SEX LINKED RECESSIVE
PAIRING RESULTS**

NORMAL MALE + IVORY FEMALE
50% Normal Males Carrier of Ivory
50% Normal Females

NORMAL MALE CARRIER OF IVORY
+ IVORY FEMALE
25% Ivory Males
25% Normal Males Carrier of Ivory
25% Normal Females
25% Ivory Females

IVORY MALE + NORMAL FEMALE
50% Normal Males Carrier of Ivory
50% Ivory Females

NORMAL MALE CARRIER OF IVORY
+ NORMAL FEMALE
25% Normal Males Carrier of Ivory
25% Normal Males
25% Normal Females
25% Ivory Females

IVORY MALE + IVORY FEMALE
100% Ivory

(Note: This mutation has to be carried on
both X-chromosomes of male to be seen,
unlike the female. Also use this chart for
Brown, Agate, Isabel, Pastel, Satinette.)

**Figure 6 HETEROZYGOUS RECESSIVE
PAIRING RESULTS**

OPAL + OPAL
100% Opal

OPAL M or F
+ NORMAL M or F, CARRIER of OPAL
50% Normal, Carrier of Opal
50% Opal

NORMAL CARRIER of Opal
+ NORMAL CARRIER of Opal
25% Normal
50% Normal Carrier of Opal
25% Opal

OPAL M or F + NORMAL M or F
100% Normal Carrier of Opal

(Must be carried on both genes to be seen in
either Male or Female. Also, use this chart for
Recessive White and Ino matings.)

Possibly, the most popular type canary among the general population is the Gloster. This canary, sometimes affectionately referred to as the "bird with the Beatles haircut," is one of those bred for their crests. The Gloster is a small, round bird, and an excellent breeder ideally suited for the beginner. It also has a pleasant song. Glosters, named for their place of origin in England, are available in both crested and non-crested forms. One must be mated to the other to obtain crests of good quality. Half of the offspring produced are crested (called coronas) and half are not (consorts). This is true for all crested varieties such as the Norwich, Columbus Fancy, Belgian Fancy, and Hartz. Breeding a crested bird to another crested bird invariably produces defective crests and bald spots while breeding two non-crested birds will produce all non-crested offspring.

Type birds are available in all naturally evolved colors, for example, yellow, white, green, and variegated. All with the exception of a few cannot have any red in their background nor can they be color fed to be allowed to be shown in bird shows. One of the oldest breeds, the lizard, is bred for the spangled effect of its feathers. This bird is allowed to be color fed as are the Yorkshire and Stafford. The latter is a fairly recent arrival on the canary scene. Although it is bred and shown to all classifications of red ground lipochrome and melanin canaries, it is exhibited as a type canary in both crested and non-crested forms. One more item about

the lizard is that the spangling effect is best seen in its first year and diminishes somewhat after that. The Yorkshire is one of the largest canaries. Note that many of the breeds are named after their place of origin, most coming from England and other European countries. The Columbus Fancy, however, was developed in Ohio.

I know I'll probably get a lot of resistance from breeders of other types, but I believe that the Border is probably the most popular bird to be exhibited. It is larger than most type canaries and bred for roundness of head and body. It has a loud, choppy song.

Another popular type canary is the Fife Fancy, sometimes called a miniature Border in that it is similar to the Border in configuration but much smaller. It is also recommended for the beginning breeder or pet owner. Others are the Norwich and Hartz. The Norwich is another large bird and is often called a "feather pillow" because of the bulk of its feathering. The Hartz is often referred to as a common canary but is also bred to specific standards. It is a good singer and easy to care for.

There are two very interesting type varieties. The first is the frill, which has feathers coming out and curling back. I enjoy the Parisian Frill, which has a full complement of feathers that are "frilled" out over most of its body and head. The second variety consists of the Belgian Fancy and the Scot Fancy. The Belgian is a long, thin, and snake-like bird that is

bred and trained to stand hunched over in its perched position. Similar to the Belgian Fancy is the Scot Fancy. This bird is bred and trained to have a body that is "long and tapering and curved in the form of a half circle, convex above and concave below" per the judging standard. The Southern Frill is essentially a combination of a Belgian Fancy and a Frill; that is, it is hunched over and possesses the frill feathering.

Lastly, there is the Lancashire, a crested bird (called "Coppy") and also the largest canary and one of the most difficult to obtain. A group of breeders has formed "The Old Varieties Association" whose purpose is to propagate the Lancashire and other type canaries that have lost their popularity.

Where do you see these birds? I generally suggest attending a bird show where most if not all of these varieties can be viewed.

SONGSTERS

Originally captured from the wild for their singing abilities, "song" canaries can be further divided into Rollers and singers. Rollers always have been considered the opera singers of the canary world. Examples of these are Rollers and Waterslagers. The American Singer Canary is a line-bred bird of Roller and "Border" parentage. This controlled breeding provides singers combining the graceful song of the Roller and the loudness of the Border. Another canary bred for its song is the Spanish Timbrado.

Bird Clubs

LOCATING AND JOINING A BIRD CLUB

If you enjoy your canary and would like to take pet ownership up another notch, perhaps even to breed canaries, you may want to join a bird club. These clubs consist of pet owners, breeders, and even veterinarians who meet regularly to discuss the care, breeding, and exhibiting of birds. They often publish educational materials obtained from members and other sources. A bird club is a great source of information on birds and can be an enjoyable social experience. Almost every large metropolitan area has one. You will probably find one nearby in the following list, which is alphabetically sorted first by state and then by club name. Because of space restrictions, address and phone information cannot be listed.

ALABAMA:

Bi-State Avicultural Association, Smiths; Central Alabama Avicultural Society, Equality; Heart of Dixie Bird Club, Mobile; Red Mountain Budgerigar Society, Gadsen; Rocket City Cage Bird Club, Huntsville; South Alabama Cage Bird Society, Bay Minette; Wiregrass Cage Bird Club, Dothan.

ALASKA:

Alaska Bird Club, Anchorage.

ARIZONA:

Arizona Avian Breeders Assoc., Glendale; Arizona Aviculture Society, Phoenix; Arizona Budgerigar Society, Phoenix; Arizona Seed Crackers Society, Mesa; Avicultural Society of Tucson, Tucson; Central Coast Avicultural Soc., Paso Robles; Southern Arizona Budgerigar Soc., Tucson; Tropical Bird Fanciers, Lake Havasu.

ARKANSAS:

Cage Bird Fanciers of the Ozarks, W. Fork;

CALIFORNIA:

Amador Bird Club, Ion; Aviary Association of Kern, Bakersfield; Avicultural Association of San Francisco; Aviculture Society of America, Riverside; Big Valley BEC, Sanger; Budgerigar Research Assoc., Los Angeles; Budgie Fanciers of San Diego County, El Cajon; Butte County Bird Club, Sacramento; Capitol City Bird Society, Sacramento; Central California Avian Society, Fresno; Central California Cage Bird Club, Modesto; Central Coast Avicultural Soc., Paso Robles; Coastal Avian Society, Soquel; Exotic Bird Breeders Assoc. of America, Riverbank; Fresno Canary & Finch Club, Madera; Gold County Bird Society, Shingle Springs; Golden Gate Avian Society, Livermore; Golden W. Budgerigar Society, Placerville; Great Western Budgerigar Society, Los Angeles; Hookbill Hobbyists of Southern CA, LaMesa; Inland Empire Budgerigar Society, Norco; Long Beach Bird Breeders, Long Beach; Northern Cal. Budgerigar Society, Oakland; North County Aviculturists, Felton; Oakland International Roller Canary Club, Santa Rosa, CA; Orange County Bird Breeders, Costa Mesa; Raincross Canary Club, Riverside; Redwood Budgie Hobbyists, Redwood City; Redwood Empire Cage Bird Club, Santa Rosa; San Diego Bird Club, San Diego; San Fernando Valley Budgerigar Society; San Gabriel Valley Parakeet Assoc., Los Angeles; Santa Clara Valley Canary & Exotic Bird Club, Santa Clara; Sequoia Budgerigar Society, Visalia; South Bay Bird Club, Redondo Beach; Southern Cal Roller Canary Club, Riverside; Tri-Counties Bird Club, Redding; Valley of Paradise Bird Club, San Bernardino; West Los Angeles Bird Club, Santa Monica; West Valley Bird Society, North Hollywood.

COLORADO:

Colorado Cage Bird Association, Colorado Springs; Columbine Cockatiel Club, Arvada; Fish & Birds, Etc., Grand Junction; Front Range Avian Society, Fort Collins; Mt. States Exhibition Budgerigar Society, Monument; Raincross Canary Club, Pueblo; Rocky Mountain Am. Singer Club, Denver; Rocky Mountain Society of Aviculture, Englewood.

CONNECTICUT:

Avian Fanciers of Western Connecticut, Danbury; Budgie Club of Connecticut, Stratford; Connecticut Association of Aviculture, East Hartford; For The Birds, Fairfield; Hartford Connecticut Canary Club Inc., Hartford; New England Finch Fanciers, East Hartford; Rose City Hookbill Society, Lebanon.

FLORIDA:

American Aviary Society, Crystal River; American Budgerigar Soc., District. No. 5, Largo; Aviary and Cage Bird Soc. of S. Florida, Boca Raton; Big Bend Bird Club, Tallahassee; Central Florida Bird Breeders Association, Cocoa; Cage Bird Club of Charlotte County, Punta Gorda; Cage Bird Society of South Florida, Ft. Lauderdale; Color-Bred Canary Club of Miami, Miami; Emerald Coast Avian Society, Panama City; Exotic Bird Club of Florida (The), Melbourne; Florida Bird Breeders Association, Miami; Florida Canary Fanciers, St. Petersburg; Florida Exhibition Budgerigar Breeders, Orlando; Florida West Coast Avian Society, Sarasota; Gainesville Bird Fanciers Club, Gainesville; Gold Coast All Bird Club, Delray Beach; Greater Brandon Avian Society, Tampa; Gulf Coast Bird Club, Ft. Myers; Gulf Coast Budgerigar Society, Clearwater; Gulfport Cockatiel Society, Gulfport; Heartland Avian Society, Sebring; Imperial Bird Club, Lakeland; Jacksonville Avicultural Society, Jacksonville Cage Bird Association, Baldwin; Miami

Parrot Club, Miami; Ocala Caged Bird Society, Ocala; Panhandle Aviculture Society, Pace; Parrot Society of South Florida, Miami; Rare & Color Budgerigar Society USA, Floral City; South Florida Budgerigar Society, Margate; South Florida Exotic Bird Club, Davie; South-West Florida Bird Club, Naples; Sun Coast Avian Society, Pinellas Park; Sunshine State Cage Bird Society, Central FL; Tampa Bay Bird Club, San Antonio; Top Bench Cockatiel Club, Fruitland Park; Treasure Coast Exotic Bird Club, Ft. Pierce; West Florida Avian Society, Spring Hill; West Pasco Exotic Bird Club, Hudson.

GEORGIA:

Georgia Budgerigar Society, Atlanta; Georgia Cage Bird Society, Powder Springs; Peach State Budgie Club, Atlanta; Peach Tree State Budgie Club, Marietta; Southeast Cockatiel Society, Marietta.

HAWAII:

Avian Research Association, Honolulu; Big Island Bird Society, Kurtistown; Budgie Fanciers of Hawaii, Honolulu; Hawaii Parrot Fanciers, Honolulu; Paradise Budgerigar Society, Honolulu.

IDAHO:

Feathered Friends of Southeastern Idaho, Pocatello; Magic Valley Bird Club, Twin Falls; Treasure Valley Cage Bird Club, Fruitland.

ILLINOIS:

Central State Roller Canary Breeders

Association, Bolingbrook; Greater Chicago Cage Bird Club, Inc., Chicago; Illinois Budgerigar Society, Chicago; NIROC, Glenwood; Northern Illinois Cage Bird Enthusiasts Bird Club, Harvard; Northern Illinois Parrot Society, Elk Grove Village; South Suburban Cage Bird Association, Sauk Village; Springfield Pet Bird Club, Springfield; State Line Bird Fanciers, Rockford; West Suburban Caged Bird Club, Batavia.

INDIANA:

Central Indiana Cage-Bird Club, Speedway; Indiana Bird Fanciers, Fort Wayne; Indiana Budgerigar Society, Indianapolis; Kentuckiana Bird Society Inc., Georgetown; Michiana Bird Society, South Bend.

IOWA:

Budgerigar Society of Iowa, Des Moines; Iowa Cage-Bird Hobby Club, Hudson; Mid-America Cage Bird Soc., Des Moines.

KANSAS:

Air Capitol Cockatiel Club, Wichita; Greater Kansas Avicultural Soc., Wichita; Heartland Finch & Canary Club, Spring Hill; Lizard Canary Society, Paola; Midwest Blue Chip Exhibition Budgerigar Society, Shawnee; Northeast Kansas Cage Bird Club, Topeka; Sunflower Bird Club, Shawnee.

KENTUCKY:

Central Kentucky Cage Bird Soc., Lexington; Feathered Friends Bird Soc., Louisville; Western Kentucky Cage Bird Club, Paducah.

Canaries

LOUISIANA:
Acadiana Bird Club, Lafayette; Ark-La-Tex Cage Bird Club, Shreveport; Bayou Bird Club, Vinton; Cajun Canary Club, Metaire; Capitol Area Avicultural Soc., Baton Rouge; Central Louisiana Budgerigar Soc., Baton Rouge Gulf South Bird Club Inc., New Orleans; Lake Area Bird Breeders, Vinton; Louisiana Aviculture Society, New Orleans; New Orleans Budgerigar Society, New Orleans.

MAINE:
Maine State Caged Bird Society, Augusta.

MARYLAND:
Baltimore Bird Fanciers, Baltimore; Maryland All Canary Club, Clear Spring; Maryland Cage Bird Society, Baltimore; Maryland Budgerigar Society, Baltimore; Southern Maryland Cage Bird Club, Baltimore.

MASSACHUSETTS:
Boston Cockatiel Soc., Inc., Chestnut Hill; Boston Society of Aviculture, Boston; Exotic Cage Bird Society of New England, Auburn; Massachusetts Budgerigar Society, Bedford; Massachusetts Cage Bird Assoc., Inc., Brockton; Rhode Island Budgerigar Society, Norwood; Southeastern MA Canary Club, New Bedford; Western MA Budgie Club, Housatonic.

MICHIGAN:
Ann Arbor Cage Bird Club, Ann Arbor; Bird Education & Kaffeeklatsch Society, Portage; Capital

Feathered Wings Bird Club, Eagle; DRAGON Chap. 22 of the American Singers Club, Wixom; Great Lakes Avicultural Soc., Grand Rapids; Great Lakes Budgie Society, Detroit; Lansing Cage Bird Club, Lansing; Marquette County Humane Society/Companion Bird Interest Group, Gwinn; Mid-Michigan Bird Club Inc., Adrian; Mid-West Cage Bird Club, Inc., Westland; Motor City Bird Breeders, Detroit; North Oakland Cage Bird Club, Daryton Plains; Society of Canary & Finch Breeders, Livonia; Town & Country Feathered Friends, Brighton; W. Michigan Feathered Friends, Muskegon.

MINNESOTA:
Minnesota Budgerigar Society, South Bloomington; Minnesota Companion Bird Association, Cottage Grove; Rochester Area Cage Bird Club, Rochester.

MISSISSIPPI:
Central Mississippi Bird Club, Brandon; Mississippi Budgerigar Society, Jackson South Mississippi Cage Bird Society, Biloxi.

MISSOURI:
B.E.R.D. Club of Overland Park, Kansas City; Budgerigar Society of Missouri, St. Louis; Central Missouri Bird Enthusiasts, Columbia; Gateway Parrot Club, St. Louis; Greater Kansas City Avicultural Society, Independence; Heart of America Hookbill Society, Pleasant Hill; Midwest Zebra & Society Finch Fanciers, Grandview; Missouri Cage Bird

Association, St. Clair; River City Exotic Bird Society, St. Louis; St. Louis Canaries Ltd., St. Louis.

NEBRASKA:
Greater Omaha Caged Bird Soc., Omaha; Midwest Parrot Club (The), Fremont.

NEVADA:
Las Vegas Avicultural Society, Las Vegas; Reno Area Avian Enthusiasts, Reno.

NEW HAMPSHIRE:
Birds of a Feather Avicultural Society, Windham; New Hampshire Avicultural Soc., Littleton.

NEW JERSEY:
Birds of a Feather Exotic Bird Club, Succasunna; Central Jersey Bird Club, Neshanic; COM-USA, Elizabeth; Feather Fanciers Society, Cape May Court House; Garden State Budgerigar Soc., South River; Jersey Shore Bird Club, Waretown; Mercer County Parrot Society, Trenton; New Jersey Bird Breeders Association Inc., East Brunswick; Pan-American Canary Culturist Association, Union City; Real Macaw Parrot Club (The), River Edge; South Jersey Bird Club, Collingswood; State Budgerigar Society, Marlboro; Sussex County Exotic Bird Club, Vernon; Tri-State Budgerigar Society, Middlesex.

NEW MEXICO:
New Mexico Bird Club, Inc., Albuquerque.

NEW YORK:
Astoria Bird Club, Long

Island; Big Apple Bird Association, NYC; Buffalo Canary & Budgerigar Club Inc., Buffalo; Buffalo Hookbill Association, Buffalo; Capital District Cage Bird Club, Albany; Catskill Exotic Bird Club, Monticello; Central New York Cage Bird Club, Fulton; Finger Lakes Cage Bird Association, Farmington; Garden State Budgerigar Society, Staten Island; Greater Metropolitan Gloster Club, Bethpage; Greater New York Roller Canary Club, Bronx; Greater Rochester Hookbill Association, Rochester; Grey Play Round Table (The), NYC; Hudson Valley Bird Fanciers, Hurley; International Canary Society, Buffalo/Niagara Falls; Kings County Canary Club, Brooklyn; Long Island Feather Enthusiasts, North Babylon; Long Island Parrot Society, North Babylon; New York Finch & Type Canary Club, Franklin Square; New York State Budgerigar Society, Long Island; Northern New York Pet Bird Club, Watertown; Power City Bird Society, North Tonawanda; Rochester Cage Bird Club, Rochester; NY/ Staten Island Budgerigar Society, Staten Island; Utica Cage Bird Society, Utica; Westchester Avicultural Club, Mamaroneck; Western Finger Lakes Bird Club, Springwater.

NORTH CAROLINA:

Cape Fear Caged Bird Society, Fayettville; Carolina Ornamental Bird Society, Fayetteville; Carolina-Virginia Budgerigar Society, Clemmons; Charleston Budgerigar Society, Hanahan; Charlotte Metrolina Cage Bird Society, Charlotte; Coastal Carolina Bird Society, New Bern; Raleigh-Durham Caged Bird Society, Raleigh; Rocky Mount Cage Bird Club, Rocky Mount; Sandhills Cage Bird Society, Fayettville; Smoky Mountain Cage Bird Society, Morgantown.

OHIO:

American Budgerigar Society, District No. 2, Kettering; Avicultural Society of Cincinnati, Cincinnati; Beakers Bird Club, Willowick; Blue Chip Exhibition Budgerigar Society, Cincinnati; Central Ohio Cage Bird Fanciers, Grove City; Classic Feathers All Cage Bird Club, Defiance; Cleveland Cage Bird Society, Cleveland; Feathered Friends Cage Bird Club, Streetsboro; Golden Crescent Cage Bird Club, Lorain; Greater Cincinnati Bird Club, Cincinnati; Miami Valley Bird Club, Dayton; Mid-American Exotic Bird Society, Columbus; Northcoast Bird Club, Willowick; Northwest Ohio Exotic Bird Club, Oregon; Ohio Valley Classic Budgie Club, Cincinnati; Ohio Valley Cage Bird Club, Middletown; Toledo Bird Association, Zebra Finch Association, Toledo; Zero Avian Polyomavirus Action Group, Toledo.

OKLAHOMA:

Bird Fanciers of Oklahoma, Oklahoma City; Birds Exotic All Bird Club, Lake Oswego; Cascade Budgerigar Club, Lake Oswego; Central Oklahoma Bird Club, Oklahoma City; Oklahoma Avicultural Society, Tulsa.

OREGON:

Cascade Budgerigar Society, Portland; Columbia Canary Club, Portland; Emerald Exotic Bird Society, Cheshire; Feathered Treasures Fellowship, St. Helens; Finch Connection, McMinnville; Fluttering Wings Bird Club, Mt. Lyons; Mid-Oregon Bird Breeders, Winchester; Northwest Bird Club, Medford; Portland Rose County Exotic Bird Club, Beaverton; Rose City Exotic Bird Club, Portland; Ruffled Feathers Exotic Bird Club, Albany.

PENNSYLVANIA:

Anthracite Bird Club, Scranton; Central PA Cage Bird Club, Marysville; Chester County Bird Breeders, Downington; Delaware Valley Bird Club, Ambler; Eastern PA Budgerigar Soc., Philadelphia; Erie Cage Bird Club, Erie; Greater Pittsburgh Cage Bird Society, Pittsburgh; Lehigh Valley Bird Club, Macungie; Pennsylvania Avicultural Society, Gap; Philadelphia Avicultural Soc., Philadelphia; Pittsburgh Youth Cage Bird Club, Pittsburgh; Seven Mountains Exotic Bird Club, Reedsville; York Area Pet Bird Club, Stewartstown.

PUERTO RICO:

C.O.M. Puerto Rico, Inc.; Caribbean Canary Club; Confederacion Ornitologica NAC, Santurce National Ornithological Federation; Puerto Rican Exotic Bird

Association; Puerto Rico Canary Club.

RHODE ISLAND:

Rhode Island Budgerigar Society, Pawtucket; Rhode Island Exotic Bird Association, Shannock; Rhode Island Pet Bird Club, Warwick.

SOUTH CAROLINA:

Aiken Bird Club, Aiken; Black Hills Cage Bird Club, Pendleton; Carolina Bird Lovers, Greenville; Palmetto Cage Bird Club of Anderson; South Carolina Bird Buddies, West Columbia.

SOUTH DAKOTA:

Minnekota Pet Bird Society, Sioux Falls.

TENNESSEE:

Cage Bird Club of Northeast Tennessee, Jonesborough; Greater Memphis Bird Club, Memphis; Middle TN Cage Bird Club, Nashville; Mid-South Budgerigar Club, Madison; Tennessee Valley Exotic Bird Club, Knoxville.

TEXAS:

Alamo Exhibition Bird Club, San Antonio; Bay Area Cage Bird Club, Galveston; Bird Owners of Texas, Ft. Worth; Capital City Cage Bird Club, Austin; Cen-Tex Bird Society, China Spring; Coastal Bend Cage Bird Club, Corpus Christi; Cream City Feathered Friends, Grand Plain; Dallas Cage Bird Society, Grand Prairie; Dallas-Fort Worth Exhibition Budgie Club, Dallas/Ft. Worth; Feathered Friends Bird Club, San Antonio; Fort Worth Bird Club, Arlington; Gulf Coast Gamebird Breeders, Pasadena; Heart of Texas Exhibition Budgie Club, Austin; Houston Budgerigar Society, Houston; Old Varieties Canary Association, Austin; Panhandle Region Bird Club, Amarillo; Parrot People of Houston, Bellaire; Plano Exotic Birds Association, Lucas; San Antonio's Feathered Friends Bird Club, San Antonio; Texas Bird Breeders & Fanciers Assoc., San Antonio; Texas Canary Club, Conroe; Triangle Bird Breeders Club, Beaumont, TX; West Wings of Houston Avian Society, Houston.

UTAH:

Aviculture Society of Utah, Salt Lake City.

VIRGINIA:

Aviary Bird Club of Central Virginia, Lynchburg; Bird Clubs of Virginia, Yorktown; Blue Ridge Caged Bird Society, Warrenton; Commonwealth Avicultural Society, Bon Air; Feather Fanciers of Fredericksburg, Spotsylvania; Maryland Budgerigar Society, Ashburn; National Capital Bird Club, Herndon; Parrot Breeders Assoc. of Virginia, Virginia Beach; Peninsula Caged Bird Society, Newport News; Shenandoah Valley Bird Club, Waynesboro; Southwest Virginia Bird Club, Blacksburg; Tri-State Bird Club, Winchester.

WASHINGTON:

Avicultural Society of Puget Sound, Seattle; Avis NW Bird Club, Seattle; Bengalese Finch Society, Seattle; Cascade Canary Breeders Association, Auburn; Greater Spokane Avicultural Society, Otis Orchards; Northwest Exotic Bird Society, Seattle; South Sound Exotic Bird Society, Olympia; Washington Budgerigar Society, Seattle; Washington Cockatiel Fanciers, Redmond.

WISCONSIN:

Badger Canary Fanciers Ltd., Milwaukee; Budgerigar Breeders of Wisconsin, Milwaukee; Cream City Feathered Friends, Wauwatosa; Kenosha Exotic Bird Club, Pleasant Prairie; Madison Area Cage Bird Association of Wisconsin, Madison; WINGS Bird Society, Sheboygan Falls; Wisconsin Cage Bird Club, Appleton; WI Companion Bird & Tropical Fish Club, Eau Claire.